TH ONE TRUE GOD

JEAN CARLSON

CREATION HOUSE

A STRANG COMPANY

THE ONE TRUE GOD by Jean Carlson
Published by Creation House
A Strang Company
600 Rinehart Road
Lake Mary, Florida 32746
www.creationhouse.com

Unless otherwise noted, all Scripture quotations are from the King James Version of the Bible.

Scripture quotations marked NIV are from the Holy Bible, New International Version of the Bible. Copyright © 1973, 1978, 1984, International Bible Society. Used by permission.

Scripture quotations marked TIB are from The Interlinear Bible: Hebrew, Greek, English. Copyright © 1976, 1986, 2005, Hendrickson Publishers. Used by permission.

Scripture quotations marked NACB are from The Holy Bible— New American Catholic Edition. Copyright © 1961, Benzinger Brothers, Inc. Used by permission.

Hebrew and Greek definitions are from *The Hebrew-Greek Key Word Study Bible* (Chattanooga, TN: AMG Publishers, 1984); and James Strong, *The Exhaustive Concordance of the Bible* (Nashville, TN: Abingdon Press, 1967).

Design Director: Bill Johnson
Cover designer: Justin Evans

Library of Congress Control Number: 2008936181
International Standard Book Number: 978-1-59979-521-8

First Edition

08 09 10 11 12 — 987654321
Printed in the United States of America

THIS BOOK IS DEDICATED
TO THE TRUTH, JESUS.

CONTENTS

Acknowledgements ix

Introduction 1

1 God Is Triune... 3

2 How Can God Be Three, Yet One?......................... 12

3 Jehovah Is His Name 23

4 Jesus: The Arm of the Lord.............................. 34

5 God Alone Is to Be Worshiped 41

6 Who Do Men Say That I Am?................................ 46

7 Ancient Israel Believed in a Triune God 54

8 Questions Often Asked About Christ's Deity.......60

To Contact the Author 70

Acknowledgements

MY DEEPEST GRATITUDE TO the many teachers who have contributed to the writing of this book.

- To my pastor, Wilmont McCrary, of the First Assembly of God Church in Sebring, Florida, who greatly encouraged me
- To my teacher and friend, Pastor Juanita Folsom, of the Lord's Sentinel School of Theology
- And special thanks to my dear sister in the Lord, Deborah Marks, who has edited the text and sketched all of the illustrations

INTRODUCTION

Jesus Is God? How Can It Be?

T HIS BOOK IS THE product of much research into the subject of the doctrine of the Trinity, born from my studies of many Bible teachers' and scholars' teachings (whose names are too numerous to recall), which I have compiled through my years of study. I now present it in book form to all who are searching for proof of the doctrine.

I never thought I'd be teaching and writing a book confirming that Jesus is God, because I never truly believed it. I could not find one verse where Jesus ever said He is God. I felt further convinced when these so-called Bible teachers came to my door proclaiming Jesus to be the Son only—not God the Son. I was always troubled in my spirit over the fact that my church taught that God gave His life for us. I asked, "God died? How can that be? God can't die!"

Yet it was there all the time, right in my Bible. I could not see it because I did not know the Scriptures. God truly has made Himself known in three persons.

Because I prayed and earnestly sought for the truth, the Spirit of truth, whom Jesus sends to lead us into all truth (John 16:13), led me into the knowledge of who Jesus really is. After years of floundering over this doctrine and never finding anyone who could properly lead me in Scripture to explain it, I was being taught by my Lord Himself! Jesus told His disciples, "It is given unto you to know the mysteries of the kingdom of God" (Luke 8:10), and I was suddenly, through His teaching, learning for myself how it could be and how it is that God died for our salvation. That one, the Word who was and is God, died for us!

This doctrine is central in our Christian faith. It is the one foundational dogma on which all Christians stand united in belief, no matter what their denominational affiliation. It is the one truth that binds us together as Christians. It remains the one most important doctrine, yet the one most misunderstood and the one most difficult to explain, even by those who do understand it to a degree. And yet we are told by the Apostle Peter that we are to "be ready [able] always to give an answer to every man that asketh you a reason of the hope that is in you" (1 Pet. 3:15).

It is my desire that all Christians studying the proof texts quoted in this book will have a complete understanding of the doctrine and be able to explain it to others. It is also my desire that the Holy Spirit will work through it to reveal to the Jews their Messiah—Jesus Christ, the mighty God. (See Isaiah 9:6.)

1

GOD IS TRIUNE

I N STUDYING THE OLD Testament, we learn that it was originally penned in Hebrew, and the New Testament was largely written in Greek. In these lessons I will be explaining the meaning of some of the Hebrew and Greek words, which will make it easier to understand the original meanings of the Scriptures.

"In the beginning God created the heaven and the earth" is what we read in Genesis 1:1. Here the Hebrew word translated "God" is *Elohim*. This word is a plural word. The *im* suffix means "more than one" and *El* means "God." So in the original it reads, "In the beginning God [plural; *Elohim*] created the heavens and the earth."

We then read in Genesis 1:26–27, "And God [*Elohim*] said, Let *us* make man in *our* image, after *our* likeness...So God created man in *his* own image, in the image of God created *he* him, male and female created *he* them" (emphasis added). *Elohim* is referred to as "He," a singular pronoun. That is, Elohim, though being plural, is one Being! This One says, "Let *us* [more than one] make man" (emphasis added). We will learn that God's image is triune, and man, being made in His image, is a triune being. God (Elohim) is Father, Son, and Holy Spirit; and man is spirit, soul, and body.

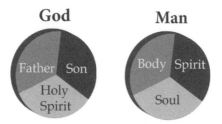

Genesis 1:3 reads, "And God said." When God spoke, the Word created. God created by His Word. Psalm 33:6 reads, "By the word of the LORD were the heavens made," and in Hebrews 11:3 we read, "Through faith we understand that the worlds were framed by the word of God."

The Word is Jesus! In John 1:1 it says, "In the beginning was the Word, the Word was with God, and the Word was God." Verse 3 reads, "All things were made by him," and verse 14 continues, "And the Word was made flesh [Jesus], and dwelt among us."

THE HOLY SPIRIT CREATED

In Job 33:4 we read, "The Spirit of God hath made me, and the breath of the Almighty hath given me life." Also, in Psalm 104:30 it states, "Thou sendest forth thy spirit, they are created." Likewise, David wrote that "the LORD [Jehovah]…made heaven and earth" (Ps. 124:8). John 1:3 explains, "All things were made by him [Jesus]." It is clear that our Maker, Jehovah-God, is the Father, Son, and Holy Spirit. He is *Elohim*, God in the plural form.

THE HOLY SPIRIT IS GOD

In Acts 5:3, Peter told Ananias that he had lied to the Holy Ghost, and in verse 4 he said, "Thou hast not lied unto men, but unto God." Also, we know that Jesus was conceived by the Holy Spirit and that Jesus is the Son of God, proving the Holy Spirit is God. (See Matthew 1:18, 20.) The Holy Spirit is a person, not just an active force or power.

A personal pronoun is used in Scripture when speaking about the Holy Spirit. The word *Spirit* is a neuter noun in the Greek, which means it doesn't have a masculine or feminine designation. You would not use a personal pronoun (such as *he*) to stand for a neuter noun unless you're referring to a person.

The Holy Scriptures show that the Holy Spirit has a mind, will, and emotions, therefore, He is referred to as a person.

- He can be grieved (Eph. 4:30).
- He can be lied to (Acts 5:3).
- He commands (Acts 10:19–20).
- He makes intercession for us (Rom. 8:26).
- He has a will of His own (1 Cor. 12:11).
- He teaches, brings things to our remembrance (1 Cor. 2:13, John 14:26).

- He reproves, judges, and convicts the world of sin (John 16:8).
- He guides, speaks, and shows us things to come (John 16:13).
- He will not speak of Himself (John 16:13).
- He glorifies Jesus (John 16:14).

The Father and the Holy Spirit sent Jesus.

In Isaiah 48:16 we see the three: "From the beginning, from the time that it was, there am I: and now the Lord GOD, and his Spirit, hath sent me." Notice the wording here: "From the beginning." This is the same inference to the Word in John 1:1: "In the beginning was the Word, the Word was with God, and the Word was God." And Saint John wrote in 1 John 1:1–2, "That which was from the beginning, which we have heard, which we have seen with our eyes…and our hands have handled…the Word of Life; (For the life was manifested…that eternal life, which was with the Father…was manifested unto us)."

Jesus said in several passages in the Book of John that the Father sent Him. We read in John 14:24, "The word which ye hear is not mine, but the Father's which sent me." And in John 8:26, "He that sent me is true; and *I speak*…those things which I have heard of him" (emphasis added). The Word, Christ, speaks what the Father tells Him to speak!

The Father can be referred to as the Eternal Thought. The Son is His Word, who obeys the Thought and performs His command. He, the Spirit, is the power that enables the obedience.

In studying anatomy and physiology, which examines the structure and function of the human body, we can see how man is made in God's image. In order for man to make or to create anything, he first has the thought impulse, which commands the nerves. Then nerves obey and move the muscle, thus providing him the movement necessary to create something. Man's thought alone cannot create. It takes our thoughts, nerves, and muscles together to complete the desire to create anything. I may say, "My hands made this," but my hands could not do it alone! It takes the three processes to create anything, just as it took the three persons in God to create the world and everything in it.

The Father is the Divine Thought, the Commander, the Son obeys and is the Divine Performer, and the Spirit is the Divine Enabler in creation. The Word (Jesus) created by obeying the Thought (His Father), and this explains why we read in Colossians 1:16, "By him [Jesus] were all things created." Jesus only did what the Father commanded, as we see in John 8:28, "I do nothing of myself; but as my Father hath taught me." John 14:13 records that Jesus said, "Whatsoever ye shall ask [the Father for] in my name, that will I do, that the Father may be glorified in the Son."

It is now more readily understood that the Father is

like our mind (our command center), which commands our body, and our body, in turn, obeys. Jesus is God in bodily form and obeys the Father's thought. And, as we studied in Psalm 104:30, the Spirit is sent forth and things are created. The Spirit is the enabler, that which causes things to happen. We see here how that God created by His Word and by His Spirit, which He personified; thus, we hear Him speaking to them as persons. He spoke within Himself. We know it takes breath to speak, and God created by His breath (His Spirit), speaking the Word (Jesus). The Hebrew word for "spirit" used in Psalm 104:30 is the same word translated "breath" in Psalm 33:6!

In John 1:18 we read, "No man hath seen God at any time; the only begotten Son, which is in the bosom of the Father, he hath declared him [or, made Him known]." Some translations read, "He has explained him" (TIB), or "revealed Him" (NAC). Our word makes our thought known to others. It declares, explains, or reveals it; just as Jesus, the Word of God, declared, explained, and revealed the Father, the Thought of God, to others.

Jesus stated that He came out of God ("out of the father's bosom," John 1:18) when He said, "The Father himself loveth you, because ye have loved me, and have believed that I came out from God."

Our word comes out of us, just as Jesus, the Word,

came out of the Father. However, the Father's Word is personified, and the Father held conversation with Him.

Knowing that our word is the expression of our thought, we can rightly say that our word is our thought. So now let us consider rendering John 1:1 as such: "In the beginning was the Divine Expression, the Divine Expression was with the Divine Thought and the Divine Expression was the Divine Thought." Thinking of Him this way, we can readily see what Jesus meant when He said in John 10:30, "I and my Father are one." And we can further understand why Isaiah 9:6, referring to Jesus, calls Him the everlasting Father. In reality, my word is me; and in the same respect, He, the Word of the Father, is the Father!

We read in Isaiah 55:11, "So shall my word be that goeth forth out of my mouth: it [the Word] shall not return unto me void, but it shall accomplish that which I please, and it shall prosper in the thing whereto I sent it." We know God's Word did not return to Him void. At the cross, Jesus did accomplish that for which God sent Him. After saying, "It is finished" (John 19:30), the Word returned to God.

In Psalm 107:20 we read, "He sent His word, and healed them, and delivered them from their destructions." And we know that the Word that healed and delivered is Jesus!

THE ONE WHO CREATED US RECREATES US

It was the Word that created us.

> By him [the Word, Jesus] were all things created.
>
> —COLOSSIANS 1:16

It took that same Word to redeem us in order that He might be able to recreate us. By Him came the first birth, and by Him comes the new birth. Because God required a blood sacrifice for the forgiveness of sin, the Word that made us had to become flesh in order to give His blood to redeem us. He paid the price for us. First John 4:10 reads, "Herein is love, not that we loved God, but that he loved us, and sent his Son [the Word, Jesus] to be the propitiation for our sins [the requirement for our forgiveness]." His shed blood bought back all of mankind, in order for Him to remake (recreate) us through the new birth, that we may once again be made in His image. In 2 Corinthians 3:18, we read, "We all, with open face beholding as in a glass the glory of the Lord, are changed into the same image from glory to glory, even as by the Spirit of the Lord." And in 1 Corinthians 15:49, "As we have borne the image of the earthly, we shall also bear the image of the heavenly."

He recreates us through faith in Him. Second Corinthians 5:17–18 states, "If any man be in Christ, he is a new creature: old things are passed away…all things are become new…all things are of God, who hath reconciled us to himself by Jesus Christ." He reconciled us to Himself through His Word.

Jesus, God the Father, and the Holy Spirit are all at work in remaking us through sanctification.

> Christ [Jesus] also loved the church, and gave himself for it; That he might sanctify and cleanse it.
>
> —Ephesians 5:25–26

> To them that are sanctified by God the Father, and preserved in Jesus Christ.
>
> —Jude 1

> God hath from the beginning chosen you to salvation through sanctification of the Spirit and belief of the truth.
>
> —2 Thessalonians 2:13

We see here that the three (the triune God) who were at work in making man in Their image at Creation are at work in the remaking of man in the image of Christ in the second birth, the new creation.

2
HOW CAN GOD BE THREE, YET ONE?

STRIKING REVELATION COMES TO us from Romans 1:20. We read, "The invisible things of him [God] from the creation of the world are clearly seen, being understood by the things that are made, even His eternal power and Godhead." This tells us that we understand the things we cannot see by the things we do see. We should be able to understand the invisible Godhead, the Trinity, by His creation.

Let's take a look at some of the visible things He made that will help us understand His Godhead. We discover that many things are triune.

First, let's look at the cell, the microscopic unit from which all life stems. Cells are made up of three primary parts: the membrane, cytoplasm, and nucleus. The cell is one unit, but it has three parts.

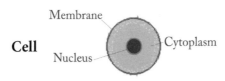

Cell

The egg is also three in one: the shell, white, and yolk make up one egg.

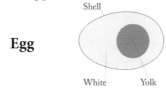

Egg

A triple-strand rope is one rope with three strands twisted together, one made up of three.

Rope

One shamrock leaf has three sections yet is one leaf.

Clover

One peach has skin, meat, and seed—again, one made up of three.

Peach

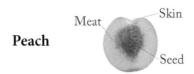

The universe is one universe composed of three elements: time, space, and matter.

Universe

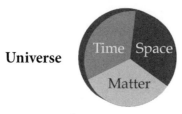

Time consists of past, present, and future.

Time

Space is longitude, latitude, and altitude.

Space

Matter is made of electrons, protons, and neutrons.

Matter

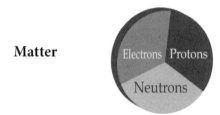

The firmament consists of the sun, moon, and stars.

Firmament

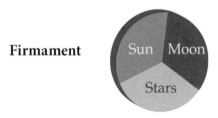

The moon has mountains, plains, and craters.

Moon

On Earth, everything falls under one of three categories: animal, vegetable, or mineral.

Earth

One day is marked by morning, noon, and evening—three divisions.

Day

One equilateral triangle has three equal sides and three equal angles.

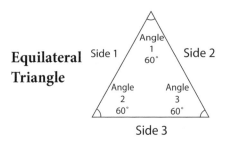

In art we discover there are only three major colors: red, blue, and yellow. All other colors and shades of color come from combining two or more of these primary colors.

In music we find there are only three major tones: the tonic, the dominant, and the subdominant. All melody consists of blending these.

Water has three forms: liquid, solid (ice), and vapor (steam).

Water

Let's look at some of the things our Bible tells us about God:

- He is omniscient, omnipotent, and omnipresent.
- He is Father, Son, and Holy Spirit.
- They are coequal, coexistent, and coeternal.
- They receive glory, honor, and power.
- Jesus is Word, Son, and Man.
- He is the Truth, the Life, and the Way.
- He is our Savior, Healer, and Deliverer.
- His three ministries are as Prophet, Priest, and King.
- His kingdom is righteousness, peace, and joy.

If the question, How can God be three and only one? is yet to be answered to our satisfaction, let's look at water, which we have already shown can occur in three states: liquid, solid, or vapor. The point at which all three states coexist is called the triple point of water. To demonstrate the triple point, place an ice cube in a pan on the stove over heat. As the ice cube melts, it begins to turn to liquid, which gradually turns to water vapor. If water, one substance, a common chemical compound and a necessity to all life on Earth, can be seen in its three forms all at the same time, is there any wonder that God, one Being, can be in His three forms all at the same time?

Let's look at another analogy. If we were to take a cup and dip it into the Atlantic Ocean and then analyze the water in the cup, we would see that the cup of ocean-water is identical to the water in the ocean. The same minerals and elements in the Atlantic Ocean are in the water in the cup. It is the Atlantic Ocean in a cup, the same as Jesus is God in a body. Colossians 2:9 says, "In him [Jesus] dwelleth all the fulness of the Godhead bodily." Colossians 1:15 records Him to be "the image of the invisible God."

Now let's look at light. We read in 1 John 1:5 that God is light, and in John 1:7 we find that Jesus is the light. If we were to make anything as a likeness of God, it would be a bright light in the sky. Let's take the sun as an example. The sun sends out many rays, or beams of light. If a sunbeam came streaming through your window and I saw it, I could ask, What is that beam of light coming into the room? Your answer, of course would be, "That's from the sun!" Now we know that beam of sun is not the ball of sun up in the sky, don't we? But it is from the sun! It's an extension of the sun coming into your room, coming to Earth. The light you see is the same type of light that comes out of the sun. We cannot look upon the sun, but we can look upon the sunbeam. Jesus is like that sunbeam. He is an extension of God to Earth! He is the same light, the same substance, the same God—God out of God. In John 12:45 Jesus said, "He that seeth me seeth him that sent me." When you see the sunbeam, you see an extension of the sun. When you see God-the-Son, You see God-the-Father.

We studied in Chapter 1 the verse in which Jesus stated that He "came out from God" (John 16:27). We can better understand now how it is that Jesus said, "I and my Father are one" (John 10:30), and how Jesus could say when Philip asked for Him to show them the Father, "Have I been so long time with you, and yet hast thou not known me, Philip? he that hath seen me hath seen the Father" (John 14:9). Jesus went on to say in verse 10, "Believeth thou not that I am in the Father, and the Father is in me?"

Just as the light is in a lamp and the lamp holds the light, Jesus is also a lamp for the Light, a body for God!

In Isaiah 42:8 we read that God said, "My glory will I not give to another," but Jesus had that same glory with the Father before He took on the body of a man. He said in John 17:5, "And now, O Father, glorify thou me with thine own self with the glory which I had with thee before the world was." The Father and Son share the glory because they are God.

In our study in Chapter 1, we learned that Jesus was in the bosom of the Father, and He said He came out of God. Jesus has always been God. In Micah 5:2 we read, "Out of thee [Bethlehem] shall he come forth unto me that is to be ruler...whose goings forth have been from of old, from everlasting." The Hebrew word for "everlasting" is the same word meaning "eternity." Jesus is from eternity! He left heaven and took on a body and became faithful unto the death of the cross. In Philippians 2:6–9, the Greek says, "Who, being in the form of God existed...he emptied himself...took on the form of a bond-servant and was made in the likeness of men" (TIB).

Hebrews 10:5 says, "When he cometh into the world, he saith...a body thou hast prepared me." In Hebrews 1:5 we hear God speaking: "This day have I begotten thee...I will be to him a Father, and he shall be to me a Son."

Jesus became God's Son as a human, but in His divine state, the Word always was God!

3

JEHOVAH IS HIS NAME

WE READ IN PSALM 83:16 that men should seek God's name. The psalmist writes in verse 18, "That men may know that thou, whose name alone is JEHOVAH, art the most high over all the earth."

Exodus 6:2 reads, "God spake unto Moses, and said unto him, I am the LORD: And I appeared unto Abraham, unto Isaac, and unto Jacob, by the name of God Almighty [Hebrew, *El Shaddai*), but by my name JEHOVAH was I not known to them." The name *Jehovah* is an English transliteration of the Hebrew *Yahweh*. "Yahweh" is only a guess at the correct Hebrew pronunciation of God's name, as only the consonants YHWH appear in the Hebrew text. These four consonants are called the tetragrammaton. The vowels *a* and *e* were added later as it was transliterated from the Hebrew into English.

In Jeremiah 23:5–6 we read where this name, Yahweh, or Jehovah, is ascribed to Jesus from the Hebrew. It says, "The days come, saith the LORD, that I will raise unto David a righteous Branch, and a King shall reign and prosper, and shall execute judgment and justice in the earth...and this is his name...he shall be called, THE LORD OUR RIGHTEOUSNESS." Here the letters in the word *Lord* are all small capital letters, thus signifying that the original word was *Yahweh*, the name of Jehovah. The early Jews would not put God's name in print, considering it irreligious to do so, as it was only used in worship. Instead, they substituted the word *Adonai*, or "Lord" (the English translation), for the name of God. Whenever you read "LORD" spelled with all small capitals in the Old Testament, know that it is a replacement for and stands for the name *Jehovah*. So, rightly translating verse 6, we read, "And this is his name whereby he shall be called, *JEHOVAH* OUR RIGHTEOUSNESS."

Jehovah is Lord, God, Holy One, and Savior.

Isaiah 43:3 reads, "I am the LORD thy God, the Holy One...thy Savior," and in Isaiah 42:8 we read, "I am the LORD [Jehovah]: that is my name."

Jesus is Lord.

Luke 2:11 reads, "Unto you is born this day...a Saviour, which is Christ the Lord." Jesus was Lord at His birth!

Philippians 2:11 reads, "Every tongue should confess that Jesus Christ is Lord." Jesus is called the Lord of lords in Revelation 19:16, and Jehovah is called the Lord of lords in Deuteronomy 10:17.

Jehovah is God.

Exodus 20:2 reads, "I am the LORD thy God," and Isaiah 43:10 says, "I am he: before me there was no God formed, neither shall there be after me." Isaiah 45:5 reads, "I am the LORD, and there is none else, there is no God beside me," and Isaiah 45:6 reemphasizes this.

Jesus is God.

> They shall call his name Emmanuel, which being interpreted is, God with us.
> —MATTHEW 1:23

In John 1:1 we read, "In the beginning was the Word, the Word was with God, and the Word [Jesus] was God." Philippians 2:6 states that He was "in the form of God." Isaiah 9:6 reads, "His name shall be…The mighty God." In Hebrews 1:8 we see God speaking to the Son (Jesus). In their conversation, the Father calls Jesus, God: "Unto the Son he saith, Thy throne, O God, is for ever and ever." In John 20:28 we read that when Thomas saw the scars in Jesus' body, he exclaimed, "My Lord and my God." We do not read here that Jesus rebuked Thomas for calling Him God, but instead Jesus pronounced a blessing to all who would believe this without seeing; that is, all who would believe that He is God.

Jehovah is the Holy One.

> I am the LORD thy God, the Holy One.
> —ISAIAH 43:3

> I am the LORD, your Holy One, the creator.
> —ISAIAH 43:15

> Thus saith the LORD, the Holy One.
> —ISAIAH 45:11

Jesus is the Holy One.

Peter preached in Acts 3:14–15, "Ye denied the Holy One….and killed the Prince of life." He is also called the Holy One in Acts 2:27 and 13:35.

Even the demons knew him to be the Holy One. Mark 1:24 and Luke 4:34 records demons as saying to Jesus, "I know thee who thou art; the Holy One of God."

In the Greek text, we read in John 6:69 as Peter is speaking to Jesus, "We have believed…that you are the Holy One of God." Some of our English translations read, "We believe and are sure that thou art that Christ, the Son of the living God," but the Koine Greek translation is the more correct version. We read in Revelation 4:8 that God Almighty is worshiped in heaven continuously by four beasts who say, "Holy, holy, holy, Lord God Almighty, which was, and is, and is to come." Many Bible scholars agree that the proclamation, "Holy, holy, holy," is worship to the triune God, giving honor to each of the three—Father, Son, and Holy Spirit.

Jehovah is Savior.

In Isaiah 49:26 we read, "All flesh shall know that I the LORD am thy Saviour." In Isaiah 43:11 He states, "I, even I, am the LORD; and beside me there is no saviour."

It is of note that in Titus 3:4 we read that the Savior is God, but in verse 6, Jesus Christ is called the Savior.

Jesus is Savior.

John 4:42 reads, "Know that this is indeed the Christ, the Saviour of the world." Philippians 3:20 reads, "We look for the Saviour, the Lord Jesus Christ." In Matthew 1:21 we read, "Thou shalt call his name JESUS [*Yeshua* in Hebrew]: for he shall save his people from their sins." The name *Jesus* means "Jehovah saves" or "Jehovah is salvation." *Salvation* is the noun form of the act of saving, hence, being a savior. In Isaiah 12:1 the prophet declares, "The LORD JEHOVAH is my strength...he also is become my salvation."

Jehovah is Creator.

Isaiah 40:28 reads, "Hast thou not known...the everlasting God, the LORD, the Creator of the ends of earth, fainteth not?" And in Isaiah 43:15 we read, "I am the LORD...the Creator." In Psalm 102:25 we read of Jehovah, "Of old hast thou laid the foundation of the earth, and the heavens are the work of thy hands."

Jesus is Creator.

In Colossians 1:16 we read, "By him [Jesus] were all things created," and in John 1:3 it says, "All things were made by him [Jesus]." In Hebrews 1:10 we read that God said of Jesus, "Thou, Lord, in the beginning hast laid the foundation of the earth; and the heavens are the works of thine hands." This is a direct quote from Psalm 102:25, which speaks of Jehovah.

Jehovah is the Redeemer.

Isaiah 48:17 reads, "Thus saith the LORD [Jehovah], thy Redeemer...I am the LORD thy God." Isaiah 47:4 reads, "As for our redeemer, the LORD of hosts is his name."

Jesus is the Redeemer.

Revelation 5:9 reads, "Thou [Jesus, the Lamb] wast slain, and hast redeemed us to God by thy blood." And in Ephesians 1:7 we read that "in [Jesus] we have redemption through his blood."

Jehovah is the mighty God.

Psalm 50:1 reads, "The mighty God, even the LORD [Jehovah], hath spoken." Jeremiah 32:18 reads, "The Great, the Mighty God, the LORD [Jehovah]...is his name."

Jesus is the mighty God.

In Isaiah 9:6, which is the prophecy foretelling the birth of the Messiah, we read, "Unto us a child [Jesus] is born, unto us a son is given: and the government shall be upon his shoulder: and his name shall be called Wonderful, Counsellor, The mighty God."

Jehovah is the I AM.

Exodus 3:14 reads, "And God said unto Moses, I AM THAT I AM...Thus shalt thou say to the children of Israel, I AM hath sent me unto you."

Jesus is the I AM.

John 8:58 reads, "Jesus said unto them, Verily, verily, I say unto you, Before Abraham was, I am." All Bible scholars agree that Jesus was making a profound statement here as to His deity by referring to Himself as "I AM." This verse contains a note in my Bible's margin that refers the reader directly to Exodus 3:14. This means that Jesus is to be considered the I AM and is not to be understood as the "I have been."

Jehovah is King.

Isaiah 43:15 reads, "I am the LORD...your King." Psalm 24:10 reads, "The LORD of hosts, he is the King of glory." And in Psalm 10:16 we read, "The LORD [Jehovah] is King for ever and ever."

Jesus is King.

In Matthew 2:2 we read, "He that is born King of the Jews." Revelation 19:16 reads, "He hath on his vesture...a name written, KING OF KINGS." The Hebrew word for *king* referring to Jehovah in Psalm 24:10, 10:16, and Isaiah

43:15 is the same word used to refer to Jesus as King in Psalm 2:6, the prophecy that says, "Yet have I set my king [Jesus] upon my holy hill of Zion."

Jehovah is the Rock.

Deuteronomy 32:4 says, "He [God] is the Rock," and 2 Samuel 22:2 says, "The LORD [Jehovah] is my rock."

Jesus is the Rock.

First Corinthians 10:4 says, "And [the fathers] did all drink the same spiritual drink: for they drank of that spiritual Rock that followed them: and that Rock was Christ."

There's a prophecy in Daniel 2 that speaks of the image that represents all the kingdoms of man being struck and broken to pieces by a stone (or rock) in the latter days (vv. 34–35). We recognize this stone to be Jesus when He comes to set up His kingdom (vv. 44–45), and "it shall stand forever."

Jehovah and Jesus both hold the title of LORD.

The spellings for "*Lord*" in the Greek are *Kurios, Kupiov*, and *Kupioc*, which are translated in several places in the New Testament as "Lord Jehovah." This same spelling is used in reference to the Lord Jesus in several other places in the New Testament. We learn from this that Jehovah and Jesus are both referred to as *Kurios/Kupioc/Kupiov*, that is, the Lord.

Going to Romans 10:9 we read, "If thou shalt confess

with thy mouth the Lord Jesus [*Kupiov* Jesus], and shalt believe in thine heart...thou shalt be saved." The Greek actually says here that we must confess that Jesus is Jehovah. Newer translations read, "If you confess with your mouth, 'Jesus is Lord' [*Kupiov*]...you will be saved" (NIV). Next we will go to Philippians 2:10–11, which says, "At the name of Jesus every knee should bow...and that every tongue should confess that Jesus Christ is Lord [*Kurios*], to the glory of God the Father." Here again we're instructed to confess that Jesus is Jehovah. It is also interesting to note that in Isaiah 45:23 Jehovah says, "Unto me every knee shall bow, every tongue shall swear."

It takes a revelation from the Holy Spirit to be able to understand and say that Jesus is Lord (Jehovah). In 1 Corinthians 12:3 it says, "No man can say that Jesus is the Lord [*Kupiov*], but by the Holy Ghost," and 1 Corinthians 2:14 tells us, "The natural man receiveth not the things of the Spirit of God: for they are foolishness unto him: neither can he know them, because they are spiritually discerned." It is revealed to those who search with all of their hearts.

> Ye shall seek me, and find me, when ye shall search for me with all your heart.
> —JEREMIAH 29:13

Jehovah and Jesus are the Alpha and Omega

Further proof that the Lord God and Lord Jesus are *one* is found in Revelation 21:6, where Jehovah is called the Alpha and Omega, and also in Revelation 22:13, where Jesus declares that He is the Alpha and Omega. In Revelation 1:8, the Almighty also called Himself the Alpha and Omega; this verse has been attributed to Jesus. Also, we read that the Lord Jehovah is the Almighty in Genesis 17:1 and 35:11. These examples present conclusive evidence from the Scriptures that Jesus and Jehovah are the Almighty God.

Jehovah and Jesus are the First and the Last.

Isaiah 44:6 declares that Jehovah is the First and the Last: "Thus saith the LORD the King of Israel, and his redeemer the LORD of hosts; I am the first, and I am the last, and beside me there is no God."

In Revelation 22:13, Jesus says He is the First and the Last: "I am Alpha and Omega, the beginning and the end, the first and the last."

Jehovah and Jesus are both:

	Jehovah	Jesus
The Judge	Psalm 50:4	2 Timothy 4:1
The Light	1 John 1:5	John 8:12
The Life-giver	Genesis 2:7	John 10:28
The Shepherd	Psalm 23:1	Hebrews 13:20

Jehovah God is:

- Father—in creation
- Son—in salvation and redemption
- Holy Spirit—in sanctification

DEFINITION OF THE GODHEAD

Within the nature of the Godhead are three identities: the Father, the Son, and the Holy Spirit. These three are not three Gods, but are in essence "one God in three." Nor is it taught that they are three entities apart from God, for in truth they are three persons in the one Being, God. Each is referred to as God in Scripture, and because each have a mind, will, and emotions, they are classified as persons. They are three-in-unity, making them triune. This is why centuries ago Bible scholars and theologians agreed to call the doctrine of the one God "the Trinity," a word formed by using the root word *tri*, which means "three," and dropping the *u* in the word *unity*. They have since referred to God as the holy Trinity.

4

JESUS: THE ARM OF THE LORD

M ANY PLACES IN SCRIPTURE reveal Jesus as the Arm of the Lord.

In Isaiah 53, one of the chapters telling all about the suffering Servant (Jesus), we read, "Who hath believed our report? and to whom is the arm of the LORD revealed? For he shall grow up before him as a tender plant" (vv. 1–2). This verse goes on to tell of His sorrows; His sufferings, having our sins laid upon Him; and His final victory. Here the marginal reference in my Bible refers the reader to John 12:37–38, confirming the Arm of the Lord to be Jesus.

> The year of my redeemed is come…I looked, and there was none to help…therefore mine own arm brought salvation unto me.
> —ISAIAH 63:4–5

> And he saw that there was no man and wondered that there was no intercessor: therefore his arm brought salvation unto him.
> —ISAIAH 59:16

The LORD hath made bare his holy arm in the eyes of all the nations; and all the ends of the earth shall see the salvation of our God.

—ISAIAH 52:10

Thou hast with thine arm redeemed thy people.

—PSALM 77:15

His right hand, and his holy arm, hath gotten him the victory.

—PSALM 98:1

Behold, the Lord GOD will come with strong hand, and his arm shall rule for him.

—ISAIAH 40:10

Awake, awake, put on strength O arm of the LORD...Art thou not it that...wounded the dragon?

—ISAIAH 51:9

I have made the earth, the man and the beast that are upon the ground, by my great power [the Spirit] and by my outstretched arm [Jesus].

—JEREMIAH 27:5

He is one God, who created the world and all that is in it by His Spirit and His Word, Jesus, His Arm. (See Psalm 104:30; 33:6.)

It Was God Who Came to Save When Jesus Came to Earth

An amazing prophecy in the Old Testament book of Isaiah tells of the promise that God would come to save His people.

> Say to them that are of a fearful heart, Be strong, fear not: behold, your God will come....he will come and save you. Then the eyes of the blind shall be opened, and the ears of the deaf shall be unstopped. Then shall the lame man leap as an hart, and the tongue of the dumb sing.
> —Isaiah 35:4–6

This all happened, we know, when Jesus came. These miracles were signs that proved to man that Jesus is the God who said He would come to save His people. Jesus even said so. We see in Luke 7:20 that John the Baptist sent two of his disciples to ask Jesus, "Art thou he that should come? or look we for another?" Jesus answered, "Go your way, and tell John what things ye have seen and heard; how that the blind see, the lame walk, the lepers are cleansed, the deaf hear, the dead are raised" (v. 22). In essence, Jesus was saying, "Yes, tell John I am He that was to come! Yes, I am the God who promised to come and to do all of these things and to save you!" It is interesting to note that right after Jesus tells John's disciples that He is the fulfillment of the prophecy, Jesus pronounces a blessing on all who would not be "offended in Him," that is, on those who would not be ashamed to proclaim that Jesus is God (v. 23).

In Isaiah 40:3, we read that the prophet Isaiah proclaimed, "The voice of him that crieth in the wilderness, Prepare ye the way of the LORD, make straight in the desert a highway for our God." This prophecy was fulfilled in Mark 1:3, 7–8 when John the Baptist preached to prepare the way of the Lord Jesus. In other words, it was our God who came when Jesus came. In Mark 1:2, we see the prophecy in Malachi 3:1 fulfilled: "I will send my messenger, and he shall prepare the way before me: and the Lord, whom ye seek, shall suddenly come to his temple."

IT WAS GOD WHO WAS SOLD WHEN JESUS WAS BETRAYED

Another prophecy we read in the Old Testament book of Zechariah proves that Jesus is God. God said, "So they weighed for my price thirty pieces of silver. And the LORD [God] said unto me, Cast it unto the potter, a goodly price that I was prised at of them. And I took the thirty pieces of silver, and cast them to the potter" (Zech.

11:12–13). Going to Matthew 26:14–15, we read that Judas betrayed Jesus for thirty pieces of silver:

> Then one of the twelve, called Judas Iscariot, went unto the chief priests, And said unto them, What will ye give me, and I will deliver him [Jesus] unto you? And they covenanted with him for thirty pieces of silver.

Later, priests bought the potter's field with it.

> And he [Judas] cast down the pieces of silver in the temple…And the chief priests took the silver pieces, and said, It is not lawful to put them into the treasury, because it is the price of blood. And they took counsel, and bought…the potter's field, to bury strangers in.
> —MATTHEW 27:5–7

JEHOVAH WAS PIERCED WHEN JESUS WAS PIERCED

Turning to Zechariah 12:10 we read that God declared, "I will pour upon the house of David, and upon the inhabitants of Jerusalem, the spirit of grace and supplications: and they shall look upon me [Jehovah] whom they have pierced, and they shall mourn for him [Jesus]." In John 19:34, 36–37 we read where this prophecy was fulfilled at Jesus' crucifixion: "One of the soldiers with a spear pierced his side.…these things were done, that the scripture should be fulfilled…They shall look on him whom they pierced."

It Was God's Blood That Was Shed When Jesus Shed His Blood

Jesus gave His own blood, as shown in Hebrews 9:12: "By his own blood he entered in once into the holy place, having obtained eternal redemption for us." We see also that God gave His own blood in Acts 20:28: "Take heed therefore unto yourselves, and to all the flock…to feed the church of God, which he hath purchased with his own blood."

The Father, the Son, and the Holy Spirit Raised Jesus' Body

The Holy Scriptures teach the triune God—Father, Son, and Holy Spirit working together—raised Jesus from the dead. In John 2:19, 21 Jesus said He would raise up His body: "Destroy this temple, and in three days I will raise it up.…he spake of the temple of his body." In Galatians 1:1 we read that the Father raised Him: "Paul, an apostle, (not of men, neither by man, but by Jesus Christ, and God the Father, who raised him from the dead)." Romans 8:11 explains that the Holy Spirit raised Him: "The Spirit… that raised up Jesus from the dead," and Acts 2:32 tells us that it was God who raised Him: "This Jesus hath God raised up, whereof we all are witnesses."

5
GOD ALONE IS TO BE WORSHIPED

*It is written, Thou shalt worship the Lord
thy God, and him only shalt thou serve.*
—MATTHEW 4:10
*I am the LORD thy God...Thou shalt
have no other gods before me.*
—EXODUS 20:2–3
*Thou shalt worship no other god: for
the LORD...is a jealous God.*
—EXODUS 34:14
*And Hezekiah prayed before the Lord, and
said, O Lord God...thou art the God, even thou
alone, of all the kingdoms of the earth.*
—2 KINGS 19:15
*And it shall come to pass...shall all flesh come
to worship before me, saith the LORD.*
—ISAIAH 66:23

JESUS WAS WORSHIPED, AND HE ALWAYS ACCEPTED WORSHIP

IN MATTHEW HE WAS worshiped as a baby by the wise men.

> There came wise men from the east to Jerusalem, Saying, Where is he that is born King of the Jews? for we have seen his star…and are come to worship him.
> —MATTHEW 2:1–2

> And when they were come into the house, they saw the young child…and worshipped him.
> —MATTHEW 2:11

The leper worshiped Him in Matthew 8:2: "And, behold, there came a leper and worshipped him, saying, Lord, if thou wilt, thou canst make me clean."

We read in Matthew 9:18 that the ruler whose daughter Jesus raised worshiped Him: "While he [Jesus] spake… there came a certain ruler, and worshipped him, saying, My daughter is even now dead: but come and lay thy hand upon her, and she shall live."

The disciples in the ship worshiped Him. "Then they that were in the ship came and worshipped him, saying, Of a truth thou art the Son of God" (Matt. 14:33).

The Gentile woman worshiped Him in Matthew 15:25: "Then came she and worshiped him, saying, Lord, help me." In verse 28 we read that "Jesus answered...O woman, great is thy faith."

The women at the tomb worshiped Him. "As they went to tell his disciples...Jesus met them, saying, All hail. And they came and held him by the feet, and worshipped him."

The demoniac man worshiped Him. "When he saw Jesus afar off, he ran and worshiped him" (Mark 5:6).

In John 9:38, the blind man Jesus healed worshiped Him, "And he said, Lord, I believe. And he worshiped him."

The disciples worshiped Him at His ascension in Luke 24:51–52: "It came to pass, while he blessed them, he was parted from them, and carried up into heaven. And they worshipped him."

In John 20:28, Thomas was worshiping Jesus when he proclaimed Him to be "my Lord and my God."

We see in Hebrews 1:6 that God commanded angels to worship him: "When he bringeth in the firstbegotten [Jesus] into the world, he saith, And let all the angels of God worship him."

He is worshiped in the Book of Revelation.

> The four beasts and four and twenty elders fell down before the Lamb [worshiped him]...they sung a new song, saying, Thou art worthy...and

> I heard the voice of many angels…Saying with a loud voice, Worthy is the Lamb…And every creature which is in heaven, and on the earth, and under the earth, and such as are in the sea…heard I saying, Blessing, and honour, and glory, and power, be unto him that sitteth upon the throne, and unto the Lamb [Jesus] forever and ever. And the four beasts said, Amen. And the four and twenty elders fell down and worshipped him that liveth for ever and ever.
>
> —REVELATION 5:8–9, 11–14

Furthermore, Jesus said He is "set down with my Father in his throne" (Rev. 3:21). The Father and Son share the throne!

SOMEDAY ALL WILL WORSHIP HIM

We see in Philippians 2:10–11, "That at the name of Jesus every knee should bow, of things in heaven, and things in earth, and things under the earth; And that every tongue should confess that Jesus Christ is Lord, to the glory of God the Father." Nowhere in Scripture will you read that a man, or even an angel, ever accepted worship. Peter rejected Cornelius's worship, as we can read in Acts 10:25–26: "As Peter was coming in, Cornelius met him, and fell down…and worshipped him. But Peter took him up, saying, Stand up; I myself also am a man." When

John fell down to worship one of God's angels, the angel refused his worship and told him to worship God alone. We read this in Revelation 22:8–9: "When I had heard and seen, I fell down to worship before…the angel… Then saith he unto me, See thou do it not: for I am thy fellowservant…worship God."

The very fact that Jesus openly received and accepted worship, while He himself said only God is to be worshiped, proves Him to be God.

6
WHO DO MEN SAY THAT I AM?

T HE MOST CRUCIAL QUESTION Jesus ever asked
His disciples, and the one we must all be able to
answer truthfully, is found in Matthew 16:13–15:
"Whom do men say that I the son of man am? And they
said, Some say that thou art John the Baptist...or one of
the prophets. He saith unto them, But whom say ye that
I am? And Simon Peter answered and said, Thou art the
Christ, the Son of the living God."

The emphasis here is not so much on the phrase *Son
of God* as it is on *the Christ*. Peter knew the prophet
Isaiah wrote that the child born would be the Christ, the
promised Son, who is the mighty God (Isa. 9:6). By Peter
confessing Jesus to be the Christ, he was saying, "You are
the mighty God!" Also, John 6:69 records Peter's answer
to Jesus' question in the same way that Matthew told it:
"We believe and are sure that thou art that Christ." Jesus
responds to Peter's statement of faith by pronouncing
this truth that Peter spoke as being the foundation, or
"rock," from the Father on which His church would be
built: "And Jesus answered and said unto him, Blessed
art thou...for flesh and blood hath not revealed it unto

thee, but my Father which is in heaven....and upon this rock [of revelation] will I build my church; and the gates of hell shall not prevail against it." Jesus was stating that His church would be built upon the truth of who He is, the mighty God.

Also, Jesus' teaching in Matthew 7:24, that a wise man should build his house upon the rock, shows a truth that Christ is the Rock that we are to build our lives upon. First Corinthians 3:11 confirms that Jesus is that foundation: "For other foundation [rock] can no man lay than that is laid, which is Jesus Christ."

In 1 John 4:1–3, we are warned not to believe every spirit (or teacher), because many false teachers, including prophets, are in the world. We are to try or test the spirits according to what they believe about Jesus. Beginning in verse 2 we read, "Every spirit that confesseth that Jesus Christ is come in the flesh is of God." Many will agree that Jesus has come, but do they teach that Christ has come in the flesh? Do they profess Jesus to be mighty God come in the flesh? John tells us they are operating from a spirit of antichrist if they do not believe this.

Jesus spoke about false Christs and false prophets coming in the last days. We see a lot of cults on the scene today, and we are taught that we can know a cult by asking the question, What do they teach about Jesus? All of the cults teach a different gospel than the gospel truth, which states that when Jesus came, it was God coming to save His people!

JESUS SAID HE IS CHRIST

John 4:25–26 tells of the woman at the well who told Jesus, "I know that Messias cometh, which is called Christ: when he is come, he will tell us all things. Jesus saith unto her, I that speak unto thee am he." This is the one place in which Jesus came out and stated that He is the Christ. He is the mighty God! (See Isaiah 9:6.)

WE MUST BELIEVE THAT HE IS I AM

Jesus made a very vital statement when He told us that we must believe who He is in order to be saved. John 8:24 reads, "If ye believe not that I am he, ye shall die in your sins." Also, in John 8:28, we read, "Said Jesus unto them, When ye have lifted up the Son of man, then shall ye know that I am he." In both of these scriptures the word *he* was added to that verse. In the original Greek manuscript, it is clear that Jesus was identifying Himself as I AM. We know that Jehovah God made Himself known as I AM in Exodus 3:14: "And God said unto Moses I AM THAT I AM…say unto the children of Israel, I AM hath sent me unto you." Remember, when the soldiers came to arrest Jesus, He answered them with the same word that God used to identify Himself—translated "I am"—and because of the power of the truth of Him being I AM, the soldiers all fell to the ground backward! (See John 18:5–6.)

JESUS IS SHOWN TO BE EL SHADDAI, GOD ALMIGHTY

In Genesis 17:1, Jehovah God made Himself known as El Shaddai.

> The LORD appeared to Abram, and said unto him, I am the Almighty God [El Shaddai].

El Shaddai in Hebrew means the "all-sufficient God; the Breasted One (or nourisher)." The word *shad* means "breast." Jesus is portrayed as the Breasted One (symbolically) in Revelation 1:13: "One like unto the Son of man [Jesus], clothed with a garment down to the foot, and girt about the paps with a golden girdle." The word *paps* is the Greek word for "breast," the only word in Greek that specifically refers to milk-giving or nourishing organs. Jesus is El Shaddai, the Breasted One, our nourisher.*

> The Lamb which is in the midst of the throne shall feed them and shall lead them unto living fountains of waters.
> —REVELATION 7:17

---

* Walter A. Elwell, ed., *Baker Encyclopedia of the Bible* (Detroit, MI: Baker Book Group, 1988); Nathan J. Stone, *The Names of God* (Chicago, IL: Moody Publishers, 1996).

JESUS AND GOD SPOKE IN PARABLES

Jehovah God spoke in Psalm 78:1–2, "O my people… incline your ears…I will open my mouth in a parable: I will utter dark sayings [secrets] of old." The marginal reference in my Bible sends us to Matthew 13:34–35, which says, "All these things spake Jesus unto the multitude in parables…That it might be fulfilled which was spoken by the prophet, saying, I will open my mouth in parables; I will utter things which have been kept secret." This tells us that it was Jesus who was speaking in the Psalm. Looking further at Jesus' identity, we see that He is the power and the wisdom of God, as we read in 1 Corinthians 1:23–24: "We preach Christ crucified…unto them which are called…Christ the power of God, and the wisdom of God."

HE IS THE LIFE OF GOD

In John 14:6 we read, "Jesus saith unto him, I am the way, the truth and the life," and in John 11:25 we read that He declared, "I am the resurrection, and the life." In 1 John 1:2 we read that, "The life was manifested…that eternal life, which was with the Father, and was manifested unto us."

He Is the Light of God

In John 1:6–8 we read that "John…came…to bear witness of the Light [Jesus], that all men through him might believe."

He Is the Very Love of God

Paul wrote in Romans 8:39 that nothing "shall be able to separate us from the love of God, which is in Christ Jesus." Jesus is love, life, and light.

A powerful thought comes through when we read Jesus' words in Mark 9:37: "Whosoever shall receive me, receiveth not me, but him that sent me." Think about what Jesus is saying: whoever receives Him, receives not just Jesus, but God! Remember Jesus, the man, is the body of God. In Him dwelt all the fullness of God bodily (Col. 2:9). John 12:44–45 says, "He that believeth on me, believeth not on me, but on him that sent me. And he that seeth me seeth him." Here again, Jesus is saying, he that believes on Christ, believes not just on Him, but on God; and he that sees Christ, sees God.

Believing in Jesus Is Believing in God

We need to read John 5:24 after reading John 3:16, which reads, "For God so loved the world, that he gave his only begotten Son, that whosoever believeth in him [Jesus] should not perish, but have everlasting life." In John 5:24

Jesus said, "He that heareth my word, and believeth on him [God] that sent me, hath everlasting life." We find in this a resounding truth: when we believe on Jesus, we are believing on God.

TO HAVE JESUS IS TO HAVE GOD

In 1 John 2:23 we read, "Whosoever denieth the Son, the same hath not the Father...he that acknowledgeth the Son hath the Father also." And in 2 John 1:9 we read that whoever "abideth not in the doctrine of Christ, hath not God. He that abideth in the doctrine of Christ, he hath both the Father and the Son." Furthermore, Jesus said in John 15:23, "He that hateth me hateth my Father also."

HONOR THE SON; HONOR THE FATHER

John 5:23 reads, "All men should honour the Son, even as they honour the Father. He that honoureth not the Son honoureth not the Father." Here the Greek says, "according as" they honor the Father, or in "the same [way] as."

THE FATHER AND SON ARE THE TRUE GOD

First John 5:20 reads, "And we know that the Son of God is come, and hath given us an understanding, that we may know Him that is true, and we are in him that is true, even in his Son Jesus Christ. This is the true God, and eternal life." The word *even* is not in the Greek manuscript. The last part of this verse correctly reads, according to the Koine Greek translation, "We are in the true One, in the Son of him, Jesus Christ. This is the true God and life everlasting."

WHO IS COMING TO RECEIVE US UNTO HIMSELF?

Jehovah God will come. Isaiah 40:10 reads, "Behold, the Lord GOD will come...his reward is with him." Also, Jesus will come, as seen in Revelation 22:12: "Behold, I come quickly; and my reward is with me."

Jehovah comes "with all the saints," as seen in Zechariah 14:5: "And the LORD my God shall come, and all the saints with thee." Jesus also comes "with all the saints," as seen in 1 Thessalonians 3:13: "At the coming of our Lord Jesus Christ with all his saints."

Finally, in Titus 2:13–14 we read, "Looking for that blessed hope, and the glorious appearing of the great God and our Saviour Jesus Christ; Who gave himself for us." Who is coming? The almighty God.

> Behold, your God will come.
>
> —ISAIAH 35:4

> The grace of the Lord Jesus Christ, the love of God, and the communion of the Holy Ghost, be with you all.
>
> —2 CORINTHIANS 13:14

7
ANCIENT ISRAEL BELIEVED IN A TRIUNE GOD

ﾠE ARE TOLD THAT the people of ancient Israel, who were the only monotheists (worshipers of one God) in their era, had the perception of God as being a united Being. This was, of course, reflected in the nature of one of the words used to refer to God, *Elohim*.

ISRAEL'S *SHAMA*

For centuries, pious Jews have twice daily repeated in worship what is called their *Shama*. This is a call to listen up, and the word literally means "hear," "to listen," and "to obey." Some view it as their creed. It is found in Deuteronomy 6:4, where we read: "Hear, O Israel, The LORD our God is one LORD."

Take a close look at the Hebrew words and their meanings in this verse. The title *Lord* in that passage is actually His name, Jehovah (the tetragrammaton), and the word translated "God" is actually *Elohim*, which, we have established already, is a plural noun. The word translated "one" is *echad*, and its meaning is "a united one." It refers to a plural subject. So, properly reading this verse in its Hebrew rendering, we read: "Hear, O Israel, Jehovah our God [plural], is a united Jehovah."

The Hebrew language uses two different words for "one." The first is *echad*, and the other word is *yacid*, which means "an absolute one," referring to a singular subject. We have another example of the word *echad* in Genesis 2:24: "Therefore shall a man leave his father and his mother, and shall cleave unto his wife: and they shall be one [*echad*] flesh." Jesus quoted this verse in Matthew 19:5, and went on to say in verse 6, "They are no more twain [two, separate], but one flesh." The Father and Son are not two Gods; they are together one, *echad*, God.

Israel's *Shama*, as we stated, uses the word *echad*, which refers to God as a united entity!

> Hear, O Israel, Jehovah, our [plural] God is one, united Jehovah.
>
> —DEUTERONOMY 6:4
> AUTHOR'S TRANSLATION

Moses Maimonides, a Jewish scholar and philosopher, came on the scene in Israel in the twelfth century. Upon drawing up their thirteen principles of faith, he mistakenly used the word *yacid* in the *Shama* instead of the word *echad*. The truth that God is *echad*, one united Being (*Elohim*), didn't ever seem to catch the attention of the Hebrews for correction, and they have used the word *yacid* in recording the *Shama* ever since.

THE HEBREW LETTER *SHIN* IS USED TO REPRESENT THE TRUE GOD

Our statement that ancient Israel believed God to be triune is also supported by the fact that Israel had used the *shin* as a symbol for *Elohim*. The *shin* is a letter in the Hebrew alphabet that looks similar to our *W*. It is drawn as one horizontal line with three perpendicular strokes upward.

It is said that the Jews would greet one another with a raised hand, holding up three fingers in the air to represent this symbol. This meant, "The Lord *Elohim* bless you." It was also many times put into print in their letters to one another as a sign of blessing.

The triangle was also an important Jewish symbol. The equilateral triangle, as we learned in lesson two, has three equal sides. Israel's symbol, the Star of David, which consists of two opposing triangles joined together, has a variety of meanings. It is said that it represents God united with man. The two triangles are joined together by holding one triangle with one point downward and holding another triangle under the first with one point upward. When moving the one on top of the other, we see the Star of David appear.

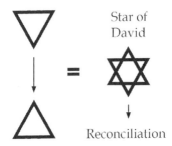

God's desire is to be reconciled with man, and man has an innate yearning to unite with his God. The teaching goes that the triangle that points downward stands for God pointing down to His creation. The second, pointing upward, stands for man pointing up to his God. We know that man is triune: spirit, soul, and body. Likewise, God is triune: Father, Son, and Holy Spirit. The born-again Jew understands that the spiritual meaning of their Star of David is to illustrate that Christ's mission is atonement. His sacrifice brings us back together with our God. In fact, our ministry—that of the body of Christ—is the ministry of reconciliation, as we read in 2 Corinthians 5:18: "All things are of God, who hath reconciled us to himself by Jesus Christ, and hath given us the ministry of reconciliation."

The Jews celebrate three major religious feast days yearly, which are all fulfilled in the Messiah, Jesus:

1. Passover—This celebration is the commemoration of the salvation of the Jews when the death angel passed over them in Egypt. They were saved by having the blood of a spotless lamb on their doorposts. Jesus was crucified on the very day of the Passover celebration, and we claim His shed blood for our salvation.

2. Pentecost—The word *Pentecost* means "fifty." The Jews celebrated the Feast of Firstfruits after Passover as a day of thanksgiving for an anticipated grain harvest. Pentecost fell exactly fifty days after Jesus was offered on the Passover, and He was the firstfruits of the outpouring of the Holy Spirit—and the anticipation of a mighty Holy Spirit harvest!

3. Atonement—The Day of Atonement was the celebration of Israel's sin covering. It was the day on which God's people confessed their sins and had the priest ask for their forgiveness. The church sees every day as our day of atonement because we may confess our sins and ask Jesus for forgiveness. As the priest was Israel's mediator between them and Jehovah-God, Jesus, our High Priest, is the Mediator between us and God.

It is very important to remember that Jesus has three

offices: Prophet, Priest, and King. He fulfilled His office as Prophet while here on Earth, He is fulfilling His office now as Priest in the heavenlies, and He will forever be our reigning King when He returns. In His priestly office He is referred to as "the man Christ Jesus," as the priests were all men. As reigning King, He is our God forever!

The LORD [Jehovah] is King for ever and ever.
—PSALM 10:16

The Feast of Tabernacles followed the Day of Atonement. This feast was celebrated with much joy. During this feast, the children of Israel anticipated the nation's entrance into the fullness of God's promised kingdom blessings. It, too, has its fulfillment in the church age. Christians are now anticipating the fulfillment of the promises and our entrance into His eternal kingdom and blessings.

Even the furnishings in the Old Testament sanctuary, as well as the elements in the Passover service, all speak of Jesus and His finished work!

Many Jews today are awakening to the truth of who Jesus is and recognizing Him to be their Messiah. We all need to be able to explain the good news to the Jews and to "whosoever [else] will" listen. It is imperative that all hear the message.

Shama, Israel. *Shama*, everyone!

8

QUESTIONS OFTEN ASKED ABOUT CHRIST'S DEITY

B ECAUSE OUR TRANSLATIONS DO not always convey the proper thought according to the meaning of the original languages, many people are confused and have doubts when reading some of the passages pertaining to the deity of Christ. For this reason the Christian cults, teaching falsehood on these passages, have been able to draw many into their man-made organizations. Some have been led astray by false doctrine to believe "another Christ…and another gospel," which Paul warned us about in 2 Corinthians 11:4. Paul said some would be coming to us preaching another Jesus and another gospel than that which he had preached. He went on to say that these doctrines are from another Spirit, one other than that which they had accepted. In Galatians 1:7, Paul tells us these people "pervert the gospel of Christ." Verse 8 continues, "But though we, or an angel from heaven, preach any other gospel unto you than that ye have received, let him be accursed."

The problem lies in the fact that many Christians are not grounded in the Word. Many of our churches have fallen short in teaching the true gospel and explaining biblical truths in a way in which the Christian can be a witness for the truth, especially the truth of who Jesus really is. All of the cults teach "another Jesus," perverting the simple truth that Jesus, the Word made flesh, is Jehovah God who came to Earth to save His people from sin and death.

In an effort to clear up any confusion, I have compiled Christian, biblical responses to some of the potentially hard-to-understand verses that have been perverted by cults.

How can you say Jesus is God when the Bible plainly teaches He prays to God?

This has already been answered in our lesson from Chapter 2, which showed God to be Father, Son, and Holy Spirit—three persons in the one Being.

Remember, when He prayed, Jesus the Son was talking to God the Father from His position as Son of man on Earth. He left His God form and took on the form of a man. (See Philippians 2:5–8.) He was always the Word of God, but He became the man Jesus. (See John 1:1, 14.) As man, He is seen praying to the Father, just as we do.

John 14:28 records that Jesus said, "My Father is greater than I," and 1 Corinthians 11:3 says, "The head of Christ is God."

The Greek word translated "greater" in John 14:28, unlike our English word, does not mean "bigger, better, or more valuable." Instead, it means "higher in authority or position," not higher in nature or quality. There is another Greek word Jesus would have used if He had meant to imply that God was better than Him.

We have already demonstrated that the Father is the commander, the thought center, the one who gives the order to the Son, the Word in creation. In an army there are soldiers with different positions, some with higher ranks who give the orders. The higher-ups are not better than the other soldiers. They are all equally soldiers, all men. Likewise, the Father God is not better than God the Son. They simply have different positions, but they are both God. All three persons of the Trinity, Father, Son and Holy Spirit, are equally God.

This also answers the question about God being head over Jesus. The Father is over Christ because He gives the orders. He holds headship in rank over Christ Jesus.

Jesus said, "I ascend unto my Father, and your Father; and to my God, and your God" (John 20:17).

Jesus, the Word, left His God-form and became a man, and while on Earth Jesus talked as a man would talk about God. The Father is God and Jesus is His Son, God in bodily form. After leaving His God-form and taking on the form of a man, Jesus would naturally refer to God as His Father and His God. We must remember that Jesus is in essence spirit, and spirit is always spirit; it does not change. That part of Jesus never became lower than God the Father.

If Jesus is God, why did He not just come out and say so?

He did! When talking to the Samaritan woman at the well, she said, "I know that Messias cometh, which is called Christ: when he is come, he will tell us all things" (John 4:25). Jesus replied, "I that speak unto thee am he" (v. 26). Jesus was confessing here to be Christ, and Christ is the mighty God described in Isaiah 9:6. In our study in Chapter 3, we learned that Jehovah is the mighty God (Ps. 50:1). Remember, God said in Isaiah 43:10, "Before me there was no God formed, neither shall there be after Me." He also said in Isaiah 45:5, "I am the LORD, and there is none else, there is no God beside Me."

There are not two mighty Gods. There are two—Father and Son—who together are the mighty God, who is One.

Jesus also stated that He is God by telling John the Baptist's disciples that He is the one that they were to look for. When they asked on behalf of John if He was the Messiah, He described His own ministry by pointing out that "the blind see, the lame walk…the deaf hear" (Luke 7:22). All these things were prophesied to happen when

God came to save His people. We read in Isaiah 35:4–6, "Your God will come…He will come and save you. Then the eyes of the blind shall be opened, and the ears of the deaf shall be unstopped. Then shall the lame man leap… and the tongue of the dumb sing." Though He did not say it explicitly, Jesus' description so much as said, "Yes, I am the God you are to look for. These signs and wonders are done so you would know I am God."

"To us there is but one God, the Father, of whom are all things, and…one Lord Jesus Christ, by whom are all things" (1 Cor. 8:6).

We know God is the Father and all things are of Him because He spoke the Word in order to create. All things are also "by" Jesus, who was the Word that God used in creation. He gave up His God-form, as already shown, to become the Lord Jesus. (See Philippians 2:6–8.) In His preexistence, He was the Lord, God-the-Word. (See John 1:1.)

In our study in Chapter 1 we learned that the word translated "God" in Genesis 1:1 to refer to the Being who created all things is the Hebrew word *Elohim*, which is a plural noun, showing God to be Father, Word/Son, and Holy Spirit. God created by His Word and His Spirit. (See Psalm 33:6; 104:30.)

In essence the three are the one God that fathered us! It is said of Jesus in Isaiah 9:6, "His name shall be called…The mighty God, The everlasting Father." His name is called "the everlasting Father" because He is the Word that proceeded out of God the Father. He is the Word who was in the bosom of the Father, and yet the Father's Word fathered all.

How can Jesus be equal to God the Father when He is not as old as God? The Bible says Jesus had a beginning, but God does not.

Jesus, in His preexistence, is as old as the Father. He only had a beginning as a man called Jesus. As we have learned in previous lessons, the Word that was in the Father became a human. That which became Jesus was always in God and came out of God, making him as old as God. That which became Eve was always in Adam and came out of Adam. She, too, was as old as Adam, in essence. She came out of Adam as his helpmate on Earth, and Jesus came out of God as His helpmate on Earth. Notice that man begets man (flesh), but God begets spirit. The Holy Spirit, who is God, caused Mary to conceive Jesus, and by this Jesus is the Son of God. (See Matthew 1:18.) He is a man in the physical and God in the spiritual. Flesh always has a beginning, but Spirit is eternal.

The verse often used by those who wish to argue against Jesus' pre-Incarnation existence with the Father is Revelation 3:14: "These things saith the Amen, the faithful and true witness, the beginning of the creation of God." Here it sounds like Jesus had a beginning and was the beginning of what God created. But we know from

Micah 5:2 that He had no beginning. He has been from old, from everlasting, from eternity—the same thing said of Jehovah in Psalm 93:2. We read in John 1:1 that in the beginning He, the Word, was with God and was God. He was likened to Melchisedec, "having neither beginning of days, nor end of life" (Heb. 7:3).

The word translated "beginning" in the verse in question comes from a Greek word meaning *origin*, *source*, or *beginner*. We get our English word *architect* from it. Jesus is the Architect, the Origin, the Source—the Beginner of the creation of God. He is not one who had a beginning, but the one who began it all. He, as the Word, was the builder of the creation of God!

How do you explain Colossians 1:15, where it says Jesus is the firstborn of every creature?

Colossians 1:15 reads, "Who is the image of the invisible God, the firstborn of every creature." Here it sounds like Jesus was the first created, but the very next verse says, "By him were all things created." So how can He be one of the things He created? He was never a "thing," never a creature; He was always God! The title of firstborn does not always mean the first one born. The nation of Israel was called the firstborn, and it was not the first nation born. Jacob had the title *firstborn*, yet he was the second son born. Also, in Psalm 89:20 we read that God said, "I have found David my servant; with my holy oil have I anointed him." Verse 27 continues, "Also I will make him my firstborn." We know David was not the eldest in his family. He was the youngest, but God said He made him His "firstborn."

Being the firstborn meant under Jewish law that you were the one to rule, the preeminent one, the one with the right to rule over every creature. One could also receive this title through the disqualification of others in the bloodline before him, as was the case with Judah. Judah had three older brothers who were disqualified from the privileges of the firstborn because of their ungodly deeds. Therefore, Judah received the honor of the firstborn. He was the one to rule the kingdom.

Consider Romans 8:29, which reads, "Whom he did foreknow, he also did predestinate to be conformed to the image of his Son, that he might be the firstborn among many brethren." Jesus was the firstborn from among the dead and is therefore the ruler of every born-again creature. Those who are "conformed to the image of his Son" are among the many brethren over whom Jesus is firstborn. First Corinthians 15:20 says, "Now is Christ risen from the dead, and become the firstfruits [firstborn] of them that slept."

Psalm 110:1 says, "The LORD said unto my Lord, sit thou at my right hand, until I make thine enemies thy footstool." Doesn't this show there are two Lords, and one is over the other?

Yes. Here David is referring to Lord God, the Father, speaking to Lord God, the Son. Remember the Father is head over the Son in the respect that He is the Commander. David, as a member of the kingdom on Earth calls Jesus his Lord. This scripture is a prophecy foretelling what was to happen when Jesus ascended to the right hand of the Father. He will reign from that position until He has put every enemy underfoot.

When He has put every enemy underfoot, He will return to the form of God, and He then will be subject to God. Strong's definition of the Greek word for "subject" reads, "To subjected to; to be subdued unto; to submit self unto." Jesus was always submitted to God, but in the Incarnation He was subjected to flesh, being made a human being. This is not to say that He obeyed the flesh, because He overcame every temptation of the flesh and obeyed only God. He was the God-Man subjected to flesh and to God.

In 1 Corinthians 15:24–25 we read, "Then cometh the end, when he shall have delivered up the kingdom to God, even the Father; when he shall have put down all rule and all authority and power. For he must reign, till he hath put all enemies under his feet." Verse 28 says, "And when all things shall be subdued unto him, then shall the Son also himself be subject unto him that put all things under him, that God may be all in all." When Jesus completes His mission, the Word that is God but became flesh will become once again subject to God, His God-form. He will no longer be subject to flesh, His human-form. God is all in all!

To Contact the Author

Jean O. Carlson

3609 Sebring Pky.

PMB #7

Sebring, FL 33870-1699

jcarlson08@embarqmail.com